Taking Our Time

Taking Our Time

Poems by

Mark Belair

Front cover design by Barbara Amstutz
Back cover design by Shay Culligan

ISBN: 978-1-950462-25-4

Kelsay Books Inc.

kelsaybooks.com

502 S 1040 E, A119
American Fork, Utah 84003

For Emily

Acknowledgments

Grateful acknowledgement is made to the editors of the following journals, who first published these poems:

Alabama Literary Review: "Afternoon Dreams," "Shit Happening"
Apple Valley Review: "the mail slot"
Atlanta Review: "room 0"
the Blackstone Review: "The Inheritance"
Buck Off Magazine: "Winter Sun," "the present"
Burningword Literary Journal: "Tables and Chairs,"
        "Impressions"
the Cape Rock: "Wellness"
the Cincinnati Review: "Shadows"
Common Ground Review: "New England," "practice pad"
Crack the Spine Literary Magazine: "Leap of Faith"
Door Is A Jar Magazine: "His Suicides," "Ode"
Evening Street Review: "Taking Shelter," "The Veteran,"
        "Beach Fog"
Fogged Clarity: "Three Starlings"
Forge: "market," "ice," "Fireworks," "Breakups,"
        "Umbrellas at Night," "Still Life with Chair and Fan"
Gemini Magazine: "City Dweller"
Green Hills Literary Lantern: "Sneakers," "Yellow Boots,"
        "The Trail"
Mantis: "The Couplet," "The Open Window"
New Ohio Review: "Grammar School"
OxMag: "Work Horses"
Paperplates Magazine: "The Gardener," "The Puddle,"
        "Change of Season," "Filings"
the Paragon Journal: "Air"
Poet Lore: "Caught in Breezes"
the River: "Two Moons"

the Round: "The Curtain," "one boyhood"
Sandy River Review: "Touched"
Sanskrit Literary-Arts Journal: "The Library," "Snow"
Saranac Review: "the gut renovation"
Slab: "The Compass"
the Slag Review: "Nighttime"
Stand Magazine: "At the Post Office," "Trust," "the conformist,"
      "Louisiana"
Stickman Review: "Breakfast Flatware, "First Things,"
      "Street Tree," "Baby Talk," "Masks"
Streetlight Magazine: "Nature Walk"
Talking River: "carter tate"
Tampa Review: "the cedar chest"
Tiny Moments Anthology: "The Sweet Spot"
Vending Machine Press: "Crushed Ice," "Lightning"
Westview: "These Wants"
Zone 3: "The Pocket Watch"

Contents

Taking Our Time As We Leave the Stage

Taking Our Time As We Walk the Streets

Taking Our Time As We Travel Together

Taking Our Time As We Try to Encode It

Taking Our Time As We People Watch

Taking Our Time As We Try to Reset

Taking Our Time As We Nature Walk

Taking Our Time

As We Tackle Work

Work Horses

In a winter meadow
three work horses, spines
bowed, graze
on what a farmer must have strewn
across a stretch of the crusted snow
that blankets his farmland, his fields
rimmed by dark trees, the sky large,
the horses, released from the warm barn,
distant, so small, and feeding not,
it seems, on the unseen
hay and oats but—having worked
the hard seasons true—on this soft
winter paradise.

Crushed Ice

The old, downtown fish shop stands
closed, and not just for the day, it seems:

the rolled-paper dispenser empty, the shiny knife rack stripped,
the soggy sawdust unswept and, of course, no spread of fish.

Yet the raked steel display where the day's catch
would lay arrayed holds a coat of fresh, crushed

ice, cleanly graded, its crisp presence absurd but
there it is, someone's careful handiwork, perhaps of

the laborer in rubber boots always there, a gnarled man
not knowledgeable and skilled like the countermen but

a simple man holding down a simple job
he has probably worked for decades, so

ancient is this shop; a job he—unfit for much else?—
may have worked to the exclusion of all else; a job

the loss of which may mean the end of his working life;
a ruination he replays each day by spreading ice as if to

smooth—before the storefront holds yet another boutique—
his soft, chilled, unfashionable soul.

The Gardener

I can't talk about it, the kneeling neighborhood volunteer
barked as he roped bundles of branches newly chain-sawed
off a pair of healthy elms in the communal garden between

two brownstones, old elms hugged by brick paths bordered
with ground cover, their stumpy trunks, behind him, cut
down to man size and doomed.

I can't talk about it, he repeated as he tied another bundle,
though I hadn't asked twice.

I can't talk about it, he went on, my extended presence,
I suppose, a form of continued questioning, the power
behind this destruction—was the whole, now shade-stripped

garden to be dug out? And had he been forced to do the work
or was he just clearing up?—pressing into him, it seemed, the
defensiveness of the weak, complicit, beaten.

And even after I left, I heard him say, behind me, to no one but
himself, *I can't talk about it.*

Tables and Chairs

It's all firewood now, the scarred, splintered,
broken-apart tables, benches, and chairs piled

high far behind a country inn, all the dinner engagements
and family celebrations they've accommodated now firmly

past, service so demanding as to render this furniture
debris, the owner and his son, keeping a hose handy,

igniting the fire, flames swirling the mound instantly,
the crackling from within it at first spare and subdued,

then turning resonant and rhythmic as if in recitation
of its own, long, complicated story, the story of work

well done, of promises kept and promise redeemed, all
ending in this blaze through which it relives its history

of giving, the woodsmoke scent—lingering
long after the fire expires—surprisingly sweet.

Taking Our Time

As We Try to Recollect

New England

The back roads of New England
I biked as a boy—hilly, twisting
in on themselves, slow to yield
their secrets—became, over time,
the layout of my soul.

The New England mill town
we resided in—its Irish, Italian,
or (like us) French Canadian
mill hands barely scraping by—
framed, over time, my soul's
portrait of the difficult world.

The tight New England family
I lived in while struggling
to come of age—its true loves
and tensions never expressed,
much less addressed—defined,
over time, my soul's difficult-
to-express struggle with itself.

Turning the familiar body I
inhabited during boyhood—
loose, rubbery, quick, intuitive—
into yet another New England
battle site.

the mail slot

after my grandfather died / our next-door neighbor / mr hurd / a
longtime friend / served as his mortician

the hurds had no children / so mrs hurd showered my older sister /
with pink satin dresses and patent-leather shoes and streamer-
strung birthday parties / all to make up for the attention / which i
sensed even then / at three / that my grandfather / having raised
two girls / bestowed on me / his only grandson

a few days after the funeral / with the silence of our family house /
absent my grandfather / ringing in my ears / i snuck next door /
opened the front door mail slot / and called for my sister / the girl
i'd always rushed to abandon / whenever my grandfather called

but no one was home / mrs hurd and my sister were either
shopping / or out to tea / while mr hurd was likely at his funeral
parlor / preparing another corpse

all i saw / was a slice of empty interior / in which an unseen
grandfather clock / chimed once / the room / after the echo died /
silent as my house

Sneakers

A mom sat her play-smudged boy
on the wooden edge of a sandbox, pulled
off his sneaker, and poured
so much sand out of it
she had to laugh, a sand stream
that summoned me
back to the moment when approaching home
after a day of play, my mom, calling
out from the kitchen, ordered me to
stop right there and
empty my sneaks,
and the amount of sand, pebbles, and even twigs
that tumbled out
made me laugh—then grow
self-estranged
as I remembered the awkward lumpiness
of my walk home and how
I hadn't noticed such an
obvious thing, hadn't been
aware of how much, from my ordinary day,
I carried.

market

going to "market" / the unguarded / refrigerated warehouse to
which we delivered our hosed-down crates of vegetables / was the
highlight of our farm boys' week

we'd load the rusty pickup / climb in on top / then watch our hot /
stripped / briefly abandoned fields recede into prettiness

upon arriving / the truck would back up until it clunked the
delivery bay / knocking us enjoyably about / then we'd roll up the
metal door to market's inner darkness

market smelled of chilled fruit and vegetables more exotic than our
own scallions / squash / and tomatoes / lush produce we plundered
from cool / stacked crates as

i / wanting to please my mother / worked from a list that she / in
her innocence / routinely gave me / as i'd told her it was an old
farmers' tradition for all to help themselves

not that anything was missed / the bulging crates all headed to
restaurants and grocery stores / while my buddies and i each filled
a mere brown-bag's worth

but my petty thievery nevertheless nagged at me when i'd bite
an apple / peel a mango / crack a coconut or / worse / watch
my

whole unsuspecting family relish my misbegotten goods / their
pleasure sending squirts of catholic sourness through my unfolding
soul

then one day i overheard my mother / on the phone / telling a
friend about market / including how i thought the pilfering i did
was permitted / and isn't that sweet

ice

in the new england winters of my boyhood / ponds froze in the
fall / and their surfaces stayed hockey-hard / until the january thaw

then their edges softened for a week and reformed / a
foreshadowing we soon forgot / in the clash of pucks and sticks

but come spring / damp ice would drench our dungarees when we
fell / then one day it was suddenly done / the season over / the
pond edges mush

and we'd stand there / not resentful / for it was always a good /
long season / nor eager / as swimming in the pond seemed eons
away

no / we'd just hold blank stares / as we shifted our weight / and
hefted our sticks / our wool sweaters a little warm / the pond safe
to walk on / but no good for our sport

each of us / side by side / silently mesmerized / by this still /
watery / moment

Leap of Faith

Wary of the water,
I stood on the dock

while my boyhood friends
leaped into the lake

and swam and laughed
and roughhoused.

Later, after
they left, I

snuck back
to the dock

alone, the dusk
water quiet

in contrast
to the churning

I felt inside
as I searched for a solution

beyond swimming lessons,
which had done me no good;

searched by staring
at the water until

I became mesmerized
by its mirror surface,

hypnotized unto
hallucination

then to the ecstasy
of revelation

as I felt something
shift

deep within me,
delivering me

to a great, glad
simplicity

and I let this wild
certainty

free me
from fear

and confusion
and shame

as I dove
to ascend

into
the reflected,

shattering
sky.

Taking Our Time

As We Notice Moments

Fireworks

Down the dark beach, a petite
pop of fireworks
charms the cool summer night
with a low, all-white glitter
that can't compare
to the sky-wide explosions of color
in the State Park on the Fourth of July.

But it's not the Fourth,
the secluded display
shot for the sheer, sparkly
rush of it, its aftermath
not a large, buzzing, scattering crowd
but—as we return to its deepened quiet—
the star-gathering night.

At the Post Office

The old post office marble
stands stained beneath each
service window, smudged
from countless customers
leaning in to push packaged
gifts or business parcels or
love letters across, the body
outline below each counter
of a curiously like contour—
the median, it must be, of our
variety—each silhouette also
the same mournful brown as if
mirroring the scarcely felt yet
soul-ingraining costs of all our
small, everyday, permanent
farewells.

Three Starlings

In the bare upper branches
of a still-standing, colonial-era
hanging tree recruited, reputedly,
for intransigent young blacks, perch
three starlings, widely spaced, still
as the winter afternoon, silent
as a boy left lynched, stiff
in a hunkered-down way
that suggests they will
not fly away from this
strangled place until—
as they bear
hard witness to all things
here below—
they find reason and reason and reason
to sing.

Shadows

The darkly shadowed
brownstone windows

serve to conceal while
the sidewalk shadows

of minnowy tree leaves
over-reveal and the sharp

shade cast by a skyscraper
boasts of all it obliterates.

But the miniature eclipse
offered by an old garden

willow tree lures me
in to linger there, a shelter

from the silhouetting sun,
a seclusion

calm enough
for contemplation,

hushed enough
for heartfelt talk:

a shady stay
from the shape-shifting

shadows I can't
help but

cast about in
and cast.

Breakfast Flatware

Concerning
the flatware on
the breakfast table: the fork's rising
tines catch bright window light though its
handle lay in shadow, suggesting a too demanding
complexity, while the sleek knife too easily—so ominously—
inhabits the tabletop dark, leaving it to the high, rounded,
sunstruck universe of the spoon—all reflection-
confused—to mirror my pre-coffee
mood.

Yellow Boots

A small boy wears yellow rubber boots
he'll soon outgrow but for now
keep him dry

as he helps his young mother push
his little sister in her stroller,
his tan barn jacket

just right for the rainy weather,
his sister's stroller
protected

by a cover of clear plastic that also
keeps her clear plastic bag
of Cheerios dry,

more gear—juice packs and
wipes and toys—in
a mesh sack

hanging from the stroller handle,
the mother—sensibly yet
smartly rain-styled—

listening to the boy's enthusiasms
then sweetly laughing and
as I veer off

and they vanish, I see them still
slipping away in
my mind—

yellow boots lingering—
as if I was time
traveling

into the boy's far future;
into stringent days
sweetened

by his earliest—
if now departing—
rain-slicked memories.

Taking Our Time

As We Try to Connect

The Curtain

A beaded curtain
of rain hangs
from an awning, the drizzle
beyond it
silvery as smoke
in a vintage nightclub,
the hush of drops
brushes on a snare drum,
the sidewalk benches
banquettes, the solo
passersby with umbrellas
singles
cruising the town
with their guard up, some
couples, closely huddled,
drenching themselves
on the streetlamp-lit dance floor
that welcomes all
in their search for love
or what will make do for it, once again,
as night falls.

The Sweet Spot

While walking beside her, her boyfriend said
something so wonderfully amusing
the teenage girl

looked
up from her
milkshake straw to smile

which left a little white dot
of shake on her lips,
the full circle

halving and
reforming as she chatted
with delight until her boyfriend,

watching the dotty dot, couldn't
stand it any longer
and stopped

to give that
sweet spot a kiss, a little
vanilla transferring to his lips,

the girl gazing up and giggling
at that trace of foam
fluff then—

still graced
with a speck herself—
tiptoeing up for a sweet, sweet kiss.

Breakups

A brown paper bag on the sidewalk
hard by a fence held shoes—it was

torn, you could see into it—and by
the next day the tear had opened to

disclose that they were the shoes
of a man and a woman, the day

following's development that some
of the sounder castoffs were missing;

then a sudden, lashing, overnight rain
blew the bag away, only wet scraps

left around the hopeless entanglement,
laces loose and drooping, heels snapped

off, soles worn on one side
or cracked.

*

Two loose sunglass lenses
lie face down—you could

rock them with your toe—
staring at nothing

but cement
while their trashed frames,

struck blind,
face the sun.

The Couplet

We lie beside each other
in bed

cozy as a couplet
on a page,

each line
of us

dense
with both

open and coded
meanings

so creating
an irreducible collage

sprung from
the narrative

that got us here,
a conjoining

jammed with inner rhymes
and alliterations

and cross-rhythms
compressed

to fit
this two-line invention

designed as formal
yet unfolding as free

so constituting
a mash-up of traditions

that lands us—
as I whisper,

from my pillow
to yours,

our secret, entwining title—
in the lyric.

These Wants

The bow of the wooden rowboat
scrapes the beach and you step out
into ankle-high lake water
and angle in the polished oars
and pull the peeling boat
ashore, far enough so that
it won't float back out even
if it storms
and you trudge toward the rental cabin
and dip your feet, sandy from the beach,
into a dented aluminum basin of warm tap water
and leave damp footprints
on the dark green porch steps
then your sun-tautened skin
chills in the porch shade
and clinking sounds
from the still-hidden kitchen
alert you to a thirst
you didn't really notice
out in the boat, rowing
alone, while a waft
of onions simmering
in butter reminds you it's been
hours since you ate,
then you notice that the few steps
that take you through the sitting room
feel ungainly, stiff, you need, after
all that rowing, to rest your arms and legs
(and to pause in the bathroom too)
but you're eager to tell your
loved one all about your
boating adventure
(in which not much—yet everything!—
happened) so soldier on

into the unfamiliar kitchen where
the familiar back of your loved one
(as she tries to unscrew a balky cap,
her hair casually gathered up, her
lovely swan neck pleading
for a spray of rosebud kisses)
stops you in your tracks
for it dawns on you
just then
in the dusky light
how all these simple wants
now gathered to a keen point
of feeling
are the everyday wants
(and here your jar-abstracted
loved one, hearing your approach,
turns to see your tears
suddenly well
so softens in tender perplexity
which nearly makes them spill)
you forever
and ever
want.

Taking Our Time

As We Leave the Stage

the gut renovation

gene / our neighbor upstairs / afflicted first by the death / after
more than fifty years together / of edgar / his gentle partner / then
by his own worsening dementia / moved

into a nursing home for care / and his apartment / the other great
love of his life / every wall filled with his own artwork / every
furnishing finessed / was earmarked for gut renovation

once demolition began / one of the building staff / knowing our
closeness to gene / let my wife and me into his old apartment / to
see the work in progress

the inner walls were mostly gone / the outer walls stripped to the
lathing / the resulting open space / gaping like a small airplane
hangar

we stood there / dumbfounded / by the emptiness / and disorienting
disappearances

after weeks of construction commotion / which cracked our
ceilings and walls / we returned upstairs to see the new layout of
rooms / one surprisingly cramped and ungainly / and during

our scrutiny / beheld a tiny piece of gene's old wall / a remnant
clearly to be covered up / a patch we hadn't noticed on our first
visit / a foot-square of the yellow of gene's gracious master
bedroom / a room now divided into two / stingy / stalls

by instinct / my wife and i placed our palms to the old wall / as if
to imprint it into our memories for gene / as if to retain / on his
faltering behalf / this last fragment of his life here / gene who / just
before he left his nearly empty apartment / to which we had keys /
we found wandering around it / calling out for edgar / palming / for
his bearings / the wall

Air

Out the window,
we could see the flat hospital roof
with its coat of gravel
and air-conditioning unit, the parking lot
stretching below, random wings of the rambling
complex, the ICU room
quiet but for the rhythm of a ventilator
simulating breath in a life
all but gone, his eyes not
closed as if sleeping but sealed
shut; the machine, once turned
off, followed by so few breaths
it confirmed the choice: He had
no lungs, after years of emphysema,
left to live on.

Later, exhausted
by tears, we left the air-conditioning
and trudged into the heat and
drove from the parking lot, the hospital
receding behind us, our weeping
still with us, still leaving us—
as we struggled
to square his absence
with the cruel, monstrous presence
of the earth's lovely air—
gasping for breath.

His Suicides

His suicide
followed an earlier, incremental
suicide of the soul, a soul
converted, when young, to the belief
that suffering
must not be eased
but endured
as proof of faith
in God's merciful plan,
a conviction he maintained, mercilessly,
into old age when he found
the wounds
of a lifetime of suffering
draining his heart, seemingly all at once,
of all faith, its chambers, finally,
empty as his gun's.

Two Moons

I was maybe 20
in this taut dream, not
looking back to that age or
knowing I'd returned to it, but simply

20 and walking
with a friend along
a straight stone path through
a forest, her father and my mother

trailing us
separately, and when
we reached where the forest
opened out we found the wide sky

a radiant blue, one
that held two moons—one
slightly offset behind the other—
moons that a planet, huge in the sky, flew behind

before ranging close,
a planet so green and blue
it could have been Earth, except, of course,
we were standing on that, though in my confusion I said,

That's us!
and my friend turned
around to find both our parents—
who were alive at the time but have since died—

gone
and she cried, in grief,
Where is my father? Where is my father?
while the planet, gone winter white, rotated away.

Afternoon Dreams

During afternoon naps, I often
dream of death.

Nothing
melodramatic.

Just how, one day,
I won't be.

No more unusual than
a turn of breeze.

Or than a child, after playing out,
running in.

At night I dream
the usual jumbled opera

of my life, its clashes
jolting me awake.

So I get sleepy
late in the afternoon

and—needing a rest
from myself—

dream of life
absent me.

First Things

"My last thing will be first things slipping from me."
—Seamus Heaney

The first things
that slipped

into my boyhood
soul

were the departure, from this life,
of my gentle grandfather

followed by
our family's departure

from our hometown
in Maine—

so from our whole
French Canadian clan—

and from the sea
that always beckoned me

to run alongside it
as freely

as my three-year-old legs
would take me:

these first, commonplace
losses—

held
uncommonly

long
and dear—

the last things—
come my last,

commonplace
departure—

set to slip
from this soul

of exile
they made.

Taking Our Time

As We Walk the Streets

Grammar School

Through the municipal green, overpainted wire mesh
obscuring the grammar school basement windows

comes the spank of a basketball not engaged in any game,
just pounded in place in an empty, echoing cafeteria, then

an outside metal door gets gut punched open to release a
gruff-voiced janitor, belt keys jangling, cursing at the world

while from a first floor office a stretch of plastic packing tape
screaks off a roll as a phone rings and a copy machine whumps

as if providing a bass line to a class that, upstairs,
bursts into a trebly, mocking laugh, after which,

yet farther up, in a distantly reverberant bathroom, a toilet
flushes and keeps running even after a door slams shut and

all the old, hard memories flood
back enough for me to know

that if a documentary film was made
about daily life in grammar school—

with shot after shot of small, solemn faces
staring out at us—

its scoreless soundtrack
would be this.

The Open Window

A battered cast-iron building—
abandoned, soot-coated, padlocked—
has an upper-floor window swung
open to its darkness, a call
to anyone curious enough
to leap up from the sidewalk,
grab hold of the rusty fire escape,
haul themselves
onto its ladder, climb up it
and leg through the window
to explore
a whole, forgotten world
of rotting floorboards, fallen
ceilings and punched-out walls
until, finally, finding, in fact, nothing
more exotic than evidence
of the ordinary passage of time, they
poke back out the window,
rattle down the fire escape
and drop to the sidewalk
holding—in their clothes and hair—
a disquieting smell.

Winter Sun

A morning streak of winter sun
strikes the window air conditioners

of a tall residential building, casting
sideways shadows across the brick, each

air conditioner, off-season, seeming
asleep, each shadow the dark dream

of an inanimate thing, the cold
passersby below leaving white

trails of breaths that, dreamlike,
rise and dissipate.

Taking Shelter

It was just
a sudden summer shower,
no lightning or thunder, so
the young family took shelter
beneath an old park tree, each
standing with their back to it so
rounding the trunk, a trunk with
gnarled growths from where
limbs have broken off, with
discolorations from disease, with
gouges that look like bullet holes:
a forking, twisting, embattled tree
shielding this soft, blossoming, unsuspecting
branch of family
licking ice cream cones
waiting out the rain.

Impressions

shadow

The shadow
of a cragged tree stands

sharp and complete
across an old apartment building,

though my angle
of vision

blinds me
to the shadow's tree.

*

pigeon

A pigeon flies toward the cornice
of an old tenement building then

draws up short, startled by something
it finds where it was about to land

and it flaps in the air, in place, in
a flurry of disbelief; then it either

attacks or shoots away
but I don't notice

because it sticks in my mind
as stuck in midair, in shock,

unable to square
with a truth

I can't
see.

*

deli

The royal blue
deli awning, dripping

with rain, says:
Cold Sodas, Newspapers,

Sandwiches, Hot Coffee, Beer,
Play Lotto Here.

The cramped, over-lit, under-cleaned
deli itself

crunching these commonplaces
together in

the dark
reflection of

my deli-stocked
face.

*

mirror

The acoustic guitar
hanging on the café wall

behind me
hangs halved in a mirror

on the far wall
before me, a mirror

in whose frame is tucked
a curled, faded photograph

of a smiling young woman, a mirror
crossed by cropped reflections

of staff and customers
coming and going

until it empties
in the night.

Caught in Breezes

I

The lumberyard fragrance
of fresh-cut wood

carries me forward
a moment

as would an oak beam, a pine plank,
a length of plywood:

this solid aroma
from wispy childhood.

II

The construction site smell
of dug earth and wet cement

stops me: if a demolished
soul under reconstruction

had an odor—
of a new foundation

sunk into its own grave—
this would be it.

Taking Our Time

As We Travel Together

one boyhood

a few square blocks / of a depression-era mill town in maine /
bounded my father's ordinary boyhood

blocks that offered / a playground with swings / a sandlot for
baseball / a pine stand for forts / for burying treasures / and for
bottling fireflies

blocks of two-family houses that ran thick with best buddies / and
held a girl / he contrived to keep accidentally running into

while some miles away / stood the farmhouse of his maternal
grandparents / a secluded house surrounded by woods into which
he'd take his bb gun and shoot / as he put it / anything that moved

into which he'd take an old butcher knife / and cut garter snakes /
into squirming thirds

into which he once took a coop chicken / throttled it / then painted
it green

a drunk driver killed his father / when my father was two

an act / he once told me / of senseless violence

The Inheritance

When my sister and I were kids, it was our mother
who snapped the family vacation photographs.

And always, in each roll, appeared a few
out-of-focus close-ups of the ground.

How this happened my mother couldn't explain,
but it made for a fun treasure hunt whenever

new prints arrived; good for a laugh she shared in
upon discovering she'd done it once again; mirth

followed by speculation of the random shots' locations
prompted by their more proper photographic neighbors.

My mother never threw a photograph away, so after
her death we inherited even those unintentional ones

and could, I suppose, collect them in their own odd album:
intimate shots of a placeless cracked sidewalk, a shaggy

motel rug, beach sand wavy as the sea; an album perhaps
more evocative than those made up of posed shots because

emblematic of all the close-up, random, unexpectedly
disorienting moments

she hadn't aimed to hand down
as she went about our lives.

Wellness

They both slept all day.
They'd been sick all night.

Just a 24-hour bug
my two boys somehow caught.

I read the newspaper, did laundry,
checked our stock of ginger ale and Coke.

It's my week for caregiving:
yesterday I moved

an old, sick neighbor
into a nursing home.

Distraught by the change,
he sat up in his new, adjustable bed,

arms raised in front of him,
clenching and re-clenching his fists.

He'd never married.
Had no family left.

The aides, not knowing his history,
mistook me for his son.

But I have elderly parents of my own,
a widowed mother-in-law,

a grandmother in her nineties—
all of whom I visit and call as much as I can.

I'm no saint for seeing to
these small, simple, ordinary acts.

I'm merely, this week,
right now, for the moment,

the one
who's well.

The Pocket Watch

With his legacy in mind, my father, at 85, had
his father's gold pocket watch refurbished.

It needed new parts, a new crystal, and
a new fob chain, but once restored it

looked more like when my grandfather
held it, not less; this watch that somehow

survived the car crash that killed him at
24, soon after he bought and sported it—

you can see in some photographs—
with studied flamboyance.

I sported that watch myself as a teen
in the late 1960s, the style of the day

to ransack clothes and ornaments
from multiple eras and wear them

jumbled together as if to say: all
time is One.

Though the day my father handed
his father's restored watch to me—

long removed from my
jumbled teenage years—

it seemed to time, as I held it,
heartbreaking change.

the present

my mother / ever sentimental / prized christmas above all
holidays / the giving of gifts her favorite part

so my dream of her return to us / two years into her death / was set
on christmas day

she simply appeared in her chair / beautifully dressed in red /
happy to preside over her own traditions again

a heavy woman in life / in my dream she was just as large / but
when i picked her up / light as a newborn

and i carried her around / so all could marvel at her miraculous
gift to us this year / her body / i realized as i held her / even

lighter than a newborn's / a body / in fact / without substance /
a perfect hologram projected by my memory / her return to us

an event i knew / even in the dream / was only a wish

though / with a sentimentality i perhaps thought she would
appreciate / i kept parading her around / holding her higher

and higher / weeping with joy / my miraculous gift to her /
joining her / for as long as i could dream it / in never waking up

The Trail

There's the water glass
our teenage son left half-filled
beside the open book
he left on the coffee table
to check the dictionary
on his laptop which
he left in danger
of sliding off the couch he left
because the word he looked up
reminded him of the friend
he said he'd call, his cell phone
left near the cupboard he
investigated since talk with his friend
had turned to the question
of what was for lunch, the makings
of which he left around the kitchen
because he was hungry and what he made
was so good, the table crumbs
he meant to wipe off
left there because
a certain slant of light
made him take out his camera
which, after the shot, he slung from a doorknob
because his shoes, angled up together
in the hall, ended up
framed in the photo, suggesting
he get dressed to go out and,
now that he's started, take
more pictures, though he had to
dig through the clothes in the dryer
first, most of which ended up
piled on the floor just when
we came home and, startled, said,
What a mess!

Compass

My dad driving, we were revisiting
his boyhood haunts
during an excursion
to his hometown in Maine
when the discussion came up
of directions and magnetic north
and my dad
drew a scuffed compass
from the glove compartment
and set it on the dash, a compass
that called north
wherever he directed the car—
angling it around a parking lot
with stops and starts—
until he gave up on the instrument—
which he nevertheless
returned to the glove compartment—
and resumed our tour
of once-thriving stores boarded up,
of old family houses fallen into ruin,
my dad, at eighty-nine, still
knowing his way around, the town—
with the mill buildings our family worked in
empty since their closing after the Second World War—
an Alzheimered version
of its glory days, a town
that my dad
would never forsake
no matter how forsaken
for as a fatherless boy
he could count on
the magnetic north

of its clear, stoic, French Canadian codes;
scuffed codes he still counts on—
as he grows more frail—
to guide his remaining
way.

the cedar chest

our entry hall holds a cedar chest / we sit on to tug on boots / a
chest filled not with linens or off-season clothes / but with the
childhood art of our two boys

we know / with our sons now grown / that it's time to cull the
stock / and as apartment dwellers / we could use the storage space /
we even

attempted the task once / but found it overwhelming / for the art
stalled us with memories / of course / of our boys in all their balky
stages / but it also sidelined us / with memories of our own balky /
trainee-parent selves

we had to learn / for example / that when confronted with a page of
crayon scribbles / to say not *what's that* / which deflated them / but
to say *tell me about it* / then listen / and watch / their scribble
world / rise sensibly alive

then came their first self-portraits / made of big circle heads / stuck
with arms and legs / their bodies not yet visualized / though the
needs of those bodies came to consume our own / teaching us to
tackle child care / work / extended family / and chores / while
sleepless / forgetful / edgy / and dulled / ourselves reduced to big
circle heads stuck with arms and legs

next appeared the mixed media of sand and beads and glitter glued
onto paper / of clay figures / cut paper / and photo collages /
artwork that sprawled all over the apartment / coating what little
remained of our battered adult stuff / especially when a boyball of
friends descended / and we found ourselves taking a crash course
in hair-splitting / balance of power diplomacy / our skills and
patience / abraded and upgraded / by tugs of war between these
ostensible allies / in their battles of fantastical fabrication

then suddenly / true representation flourished / striking sketches of
family and friends / and self-portraits that now had full bodies /
and deft expressions / art that taught us the close aesthetic analysis
we applied to discern the artists' inner lives / as they strayed
further and further from home / and from casual confidences / an
analysis that became our lifeline / to their unfolding / autonomous
selves

then the art cache ended / for what they produced they kept for
themselves / or discarded before we could corral it / a seemingly
sudden loss / we had to learn to make hard / grudging / peace with

so when we revisited the artwork / that one time / and found so
many growing pains / both the boys' and ours / hauled up / and
exposed / we loaded it all back in / dropped down the top and /
challenged / as our final lesson / to appreciate the completion of
our own long / collaborative / interactive project / proceeded to sit /
side by side / happy and happily / on it

Taking Our Time

As We Try to Encode It

the conformist

we had two jazz clubs in albany ny in the stark 1960s / the
white and the black

one at the country end of a long suburban strip / one in town in
distressed arbor hill

each with a different audience and different stock of
musicians / but for gil / a drummer

who shuttled between both / and for me / a teenaged drummer
he let sit in wherever he was

a prickly white married to belle / a gentle black woman / gil
lived in arbor hill with her and their three young children

gil liked to brag about his dishonorable discharge from the
army for what they called his inadaptability / the final straw

the drunken night / actually three in the morning / he dropped a
bass drum down the staircase

outside his commanding officer's residence / it was a story gil
loved to repeat / his official unfitness for the military

a triumph / as he saw it / of spiky individuality / over blind
conformity

at the start of a night at one of the clubs / i'd sit alone at a table
with a coke and listen as the musicians settled in

each standard drawing them deeper into their musical selves /
each standard drawing me closer to the blissful moment

i'd get the cue to sit in / which moment i knew had come
when / after a break / the whole band would be on the stand

waiting for gil / who'd stumble out of the bathroom and glare
at me as if pissed off

of course i was a kid / and didn't understand about heroin yet

at both clubs / despite their seemingly exclusive worlds / if you
walked in to hear jazz / you were family and felt at home

for the bond of jazz was and is stronger than any division of
race or / in my case then / race and age

but both clubs / finally / had enough with gil's drug abuse / and
let him go / he lost his day job at an auto body shop too

and eventually even belle lost heart and left / taking their kids

only then was i told of gil's habit / born of his troubled need to
cop what he thought was authentic ghetto life

only then did i realize why he'd let me sit in / making me his
flunky / in blind conformity

The Library

Rain on the slate roof
renders this dry library

drier yet, its smell
of old glue and paper dust

distancing us
from the rain-lashed world,

a fragrance
born of generations

of moldy
yet cogent texts

that shelter us—
long after we leave—

with propositions
reeking

of reason; umbrellas
in the rain.

carter tate

carter tate / the man said / his southern accent / after the phone startled me awake / fixing my bleary location / in an alabama roadside motel / the rest of the rock band / down the row of rooms / like boarded rescue dogs

wrong room / i mumbled / annoyed at the mistake / as this middle-of-the-night phone call disturbed my few hours of sleep / between last night's club date / and this morning's bus

carter tate / the gruff gent insisted / annoyed himself / and why i didn't hang up i don't know / grogginess perhaps making me righteously indignant / but i nearly shouted to him / *there's no carter tate here*

then he slowed down for the obvious yankee and said / full of professional patience tested to its southern-hospitality limits / *carter-ta-eight*

i had left a wake-up call for 7:45

outside / in the early morning light / by the idling bus / stood a vending machine / and i figured even vending machine coffee might help / so i plunked in my coins for the largest styrofoam cup on display / before noticing the handwritten sign / *night crawlers*

onto the bus / i took my cup / which opened to dirt-coated worms crowded in / over entangled / far from home turf

when we arrived in georgia / and parked outside the next club / i searched behind it / until i found a sweet patch of loam and weeds and broken beer bottles / where i again uncovered the cup and let the crawlers loose / all once fated for a hook / a drowning / and a final dicing / they now all slithered away / each to find a new life

The Puddle

Spare raindrops
plop onto a puddle, each
drop made visible only through
the varying circles of displaced water
each creates, all the radiating rings overlapping
and intertwining, a responsive surface on which an abstract
artist could drip notions of singleness, linking, scattering,
and vanishing beneath which would lurk, as always,
his own reflected face.

practice pad

my first practice pad / a slice of old brown rubber / glued to a
square of splintered wood / has become / from years of use / as
worn as my first drum teacher's / its coin-sized center / as with
his / battered to off-white / a focus key to developing quickness of
stroke

mr dooley didn't pound out the rudiments he taught me / but
seemed to speak them in a sweet / easy / grandfatherly patter / that
matched his receding white hair / his large / soft hands / and the
sleeveless argyle sweaters he wore when he came to our house to
conduct a lesson

with such a precise language at his deft disposal / he hardly spoke
a word / only raised a stick in gentle admonishment when i needed
it / then showed me / again / how a thing was done

once i'd proved myself on the pad / my parents bought me a snare
drum for christmas / to which i eventually added a cymbal / then as
money allowed / a complete drum set / followed / finally / by
percussion instruments enough to sustain a career

but with my pad now a double of mr dooley's / and my touch /
too / finally free as his / i feel a return / to the pure / quiet /
pad-tapping time i began / knowing that when i commence a
conversation / in the ultimately intimate language of rhythm / it's
mr dooley / a mere medium / he once said / for his own first drum
teacher / who speaks through time

Ode

The acoustic guitars
in a dusty instrument shop
hang off one wall
in an angled row, each
awaiting, it seems, the one
who will best know
how to coax it
into a progression of harmonies
that resonate throughout
its warm, open body; vibrations
the player, pressed to it, absorbs
back to the bone, guitar, and guitarist—
and their gathering eavesdroppers—
each made more.

Taking Our Time

As We People Watch

Umbrellas at Night

From this high window, the dark ribs
of a fruit man's overlapping umbrellas

below—tan fabric aglow—curve
exposed, his patrons, as they move

in and out of the spotlit shelters,
silhouetted on the taut canvases,

the fruit man the center of a shadow play,
the figures expanding and shrinking across

the umbrellas like voices lowered and raised,
shifting shapes you could use to dream up

any number of dramas, even after
the patrons fall to infrequent and

the fruit man's shadow, through the night,
grows still on a stool.

Shit Happening

A muscled young man
in a strap T-shirt
storms up the sidewalk
and overtakes me, hissing
to himself, as he does,
"I was looking *forward* to that shit,"
then we hear
the young woman who (wisely, I think)
just blew off their date
giggle (unwisely, I think)
in relief with her attending girlfriend,
a laugh the young man reads, given
his furious stop-and-spin-around,
as mockery, though
he doesn't stalk back (thankfully)
but presses on with stoked rage (unfortunately)
toward some guy in a bar
watching a game
by an open door; a skinny guy,
laughing.

Lightning

All it took
was a whiff of rain
and some distant thunder
for the umpires and Little League coaches
to glance to one another then, as the next ominous
roll drew near, to call all the games on the overlapping fields,

the adults in nearby
softball games also dispersing,
the disappointed kids and bar-league players,
with these couple of hours already charted out, suddenly
adrift, the parents taking the kids to ice cream parlors, the aging

warriors heading
back to their home pubs,
all the players, young and old, still
in uniform, carrying gear, their dreams
of victory put on hold, the opportunities offered

by this found time
first slowly appearing
with the appearance of milk shakes
and cross-team goofing around or rounds of draft beer
and brightening bar talk—possibilities that swirled up like

the storm itself
until all were struck
by the bright, unexpected,
electrical charge of the unplanned.

Baby Talk

From where the baby was being held
in her mother's arms, the cherry tree buds

trembled too far away for her to grasp,
try as she might, her mother—distracted

by cell-phone talk—keeping her
anchored with an abstracted grip,

the baby straining forward while
wriggling and pointing and swinging

at the fluttery petals her
fingers failed to touch.

So the baby finally reached out
to the scalloped pink loveliness

in the only way left:
in a burst of gibberish

made up of words made up
to engage this spray of spring,

eloquent nonsense that the baby,
lurching up, amplified upon

with yet more elaborate inventions,
her voice by then all but in song

trilling lyrics that connected her
to the wondrous flowers while

also connecting her, it seemed,
to the wondrous reach of words.

The Veteran

By a park bench, in a wheelchair, behind
a hand-lettered cardboard sign
and begging cup, sits
a homeless Vietnam War veteran who
catches sight of a youth soccer team
in powder blue satin jerseys
trotting down a sloping path
toward a playing field bathed in sun, toward
a green arena awaiting
the coming clashes of competition, a languor
glazing the tranquil scene, the field
framed by shade trees and
fed by more winding paths, and
the vet
smiles at the sight
while idly readjusting
each leg stump; is so entranced
he doesn't notice
the tuck of my dollar into his cup, the least
I can offer this sidelined soldier
game enough to find joy in those
healthy in peacetime.

Masks

Aging faces
not only look a mask
but—especially when tired—
feel it, the sorrow lines
cutting in, the disappointment lines
pulling down, the regret lines
brawling in the brow
until
some miniature joy
provides nature's own
facelift
and the mask becomes
mobile again, expressing—
it not only looks but feels—
an inner incandescence
earned along with the engraved
grief, a radiance that
remodels the mask
into a youthfulness
that can blossom only
over a lifetime, a youthfulness
of which the young
can only dream.

room 0

strikingly non-descript / my face attracts strangers who need to
project / as if onto a blank screen / the movie of their lives

to one i was her long-lost brother / until our tearful mid-embrace

to another i was steven spielberg / her side-crabbing husband
snapping photos of us / despite my denials / which she responded
to with a coyly scolding / *oh steven*

you look like my husband looked / one elderly woman told me /
relying / in stunned confusion / on her cane / *thirty-five years ago* /
god rest his soul

my buddy would look just like you / a bewildered guy in a yankee
jacket said / after giving my back / as he'd run up from behind / a
hearty whack / *if he shaved his beard*

this bewildered *me* / i had just shaved my beard so i wouldn't look
like steven spielberg

greek / hebrew / spanish / czech / all have been spoken to me on
the street or in shops / without a moment's hesitation or doubt /
while my real friends often pass me by / not recognizing me / or
my following shouts

once / checking into a motel in a featureless pennsylvania town / i
was handed the key to room zero / and my traveling companions
laughed / *it fits you somehow* they said / not meanly / just as a
matter of fact

the key turned the lock easily / and the lights flicked on to a room
like a thousand other motel rooms in a thousand other small /
featureless / american towns

holding the key / i sat on the creaky bed / far from home / far from feeling arrived to anyplace / far from feeling like anyone / anywhere

Taking Our Time

As We Try to Reset

Still Life with Chair and Fan

On a plain
chair back cushion
rises sunlight in
discs designed by
holes that encircle
the cord of the window blinds,
the setting sun recasting, in time,
the sharp discs to soft ovals
that slide to the side, slats
of blind-light appearing,
the slats and ovals then
slipping to the wall and, finally, fading
as the empty chair
draws in the dusk
that mottles it
to shapelessness
while a sweeping fan
seems to search
for something getting
lost, blindly,
left and right, left and right.

Change of Season

Sensing that the cold
has diminished to cool, you
lift a sticky window
of the room you've been
wintering in, the room
you've grown accustomed to—silent, dusty, overheated—
and what you notice
after the rush of bracing air
are everyday sounds—a barking dog,
quiet birds, a passing car—that make you
ponder the everyday exclusions
of yet another
season of private darkness
endured.

Filings

Gritty
iron filings
swirl in the magnetized tunnel
of my sleep
in what seems
a chaos
of attraction and repulsion
that I slowly dream to see
forms instead
one hologram, a strange,
ballooning, undulating, metal-particle
self-portrait that, as waking nears,
whirls up and away
as if detecting
I'm too worn down
to face up
to the gritty truth
I must already know
yet don't.

Nighttime

I found kinship
once
in a traffic light
that cycled
all night
in the deserted
intersection
outside my motel.

Years later, in a soft evening rain,
I found it again
in an overstretched
black garbage bag
waiting
by a dark restaurant.

Then late in life, when I spied
an old, disused subway car
in a dimly lit corner
of the train lot
at the end of the line,
and saw
how its splashes of graffiti
made it seem simultaneously
assaulted and beautiful,
I had to admit
that its grace was something
to see—if apart from me.

Touched

One touch straightens
an old, smooth candle tilted
in its tarnished holder for years.

One touch halts
a grandfather clock's pendulum, comforts
a grieving friend, tests a baby's bath, tips over a wineglass.

One touch heralds
adultery, chills a child, allows
a final, expressive piano note to ring.

One touch, then another, brings
us fingerprinted entryways, frayed collars,
read books, diagnoses of illness, erotic bliss.

When I was a boy among innocent boys,
we used to laugh at crazy, mumbling old men,
rotating our fingers by our temples and saying to each other,

He's touched.

Taking Our Time

As We Nature Walk

Snow

Snow drapes the old battlefield
like a flag of surrender, the clearing's hard history
yielding, as it has for more than a century, to the softest of nature,

the land's cold present
free of the fiery grievances that have
long since moved on to new and bigger arenas,

this venerable tract now resting beneath
snow icing—as if in remembrance of the grief
that lies beyond all grievances—to a tight embrace.

Nature Walk

The windblown side
of a tree trunk stands

drenched, its opposing side
dry, the sky—

half blue,
half clouded—

also divided so
splitting a meadow

into sun
and shadow

while a path
puddle

lies perfectly
parted

into reflection
and floating leaves:

taut
counterbalances

that sharpen
and still

this squally
fall day

into a singular
beauty.

City Dweller

The elm tree,
its long, narrow,

sun-seeking trunk
rising up then parting,

one branch flung back
down then dramatically up

again like a dancer's expressively
held arm, the other branch curving in

like a dancer's agile spine, autumn leaves
half-gone as if shaken off in dancing passion,

its nimble contortions both despite and due to its
oppressively crowded city surroundings, its stance—

unlike that of its mild, classic, sun-drenched
country cousins—

beautifully, bravely
wild.

Street Tree

A hose curls lazily
on a damp sidewalk, water

pooled in sidewalk seams
to make toy streams,

cement—reeking in the wake
of a heavy hosing—cracked

by roots recruiting
water for passage

up a tree trunk's hard
darkness, darkness

that—water-softened—
butterfly-twirls

itself into
delicate white buds.

Louisiana

Clouds rounded and blue as whales
float belly to belly in the dusk sky
above a frame house on a back road
brashly lit for a movie shoot, lights
and camera and dolly and reflectors
and the dark figures of the crew all
directed on the dazzling cast enacting
a scripted story in an effort—and
we spectators crane our necks hoping
to witness success—to manufacture
an actuality as memorable as the solemn
sky the dark trees surrounding the house
rise into; as engaging as this school of whales
lowering past in the Louisiana heavens
deep in the dusk moviemakers themselves
call the magic hour.

Beach Fog

In dusk beach fog, serenaded
by low tide breakers, stands a
muted gathering that presents a
mix of ages, some in parkas and shoes,
some still in bathing suits; a pit fire
begun, the blaze, from this distance, small
as a lit match held at arm's length; no one
arriving, no one leaving, all seeming
captive by a wish to witness
the done day's final transition; seeming
held by a longing for an evident sign
of something transcendent, of meaning more
lasting, from the life of this day, than
what they can fashion from
their own experience of it,
these pilgrims
waiting in the dusk.

About the Author

Mark Belair's poems have appeared in *Harvard Review, Michigan Quarterly Review,* and *Poetry East* among other journals. His previous collections include *Watching Ourselves; Breathing Room; Night Watch; While We're Waiting;* and *Walk With Me.*

Please visit www.markbelair.com

www.ingramcontent.com/pod-product-compliance
Lightning Source LLC
Chambersburg PA
CBHW022154080426
42734CB00006B/431